# Kindle Formatting Guide for Idjits

## Taking Your Manuscript and Making it Kindle Compatible in Seven Easy Steps

Rebecca Melvin – Double Edge Press

Double Edge Press, Scenery Hill, Pennsylvania

Double Edge Press

ISBN 9781482752465

Kindle Formatting Guide for Idjits
Copyright © 2012 Rebecca Melvin - Double Edge Press

Cover Artwork: Design by Double Edge Press.

Non-fiction.

# Acknowledgments and Thanks – Introduction

Only God can ensure that a person is in the right place at the right time to take advantage of the purpose He has for one's life. I began Double Edge Press in 2005 using a then fairly new business model of print on demand printing. I had no idea that this small venture would explode into a $100,000.00 per year (and rising) gross revenue business, with seventeen (and counting) authors and over thirty (again, more by the time you are reading this) books, or that I would be at the very forefront of ebooks when they burst upon the scene in late 2010.

Learning ebooks was a challenge, especially for those of us who were at the very start of this huge revolution. We had no idea that it would bring in the revenue it has, grow as quickly at it has, and be as exciting as it is. We only knew that we owed it to our authors to cover every possible market and we were determined to do so, even if it meant learning a whole new skill set.

During the course of this learning curve, I learned a simple truth: formatting an ebook for Kindle was nearly identical to formatting an ebook for Smashwords. The only real difference was that Smashwords required an ISBN (easily attainable from them for free or a small fee, depending on whether you wish them or yourself as the holder of record) and Kindle did not. To expedite the process, I came up with a bulleted list on my computer that boiled down to seven simple steps. It guaranteed acceptance into Kindle *and* into the Smashwords Premium Catalog the first time every time (making our ebooks available to just about every reading device known to mankind at any given time, including Nook and iBooks).

About a year ago, after running across numerous complaints of frustration from independent authors over how to format their work and have it accepted for both Kindle and

Smashwords, I fleshed out my bulleted list and offered it on the market as *The Smashwords Style Guide for Idjits: Taking Your Manuscript and Making it Smashwords Compatible in Seven Easy Steps.* I was surprised and gratified at the response it received. Every rating was five stars with numerous in-depth, humorous reviews where more than one reader now proudly claimed the title of 'one happy idjit' after successfully and easily formatting their work and having it accepted on the first submission.

What I didn't realize, and should have, was that because of the title of the book, those independents most interested in submitting to Kindle were passing the book over, even though it had everything they needed to know to format their work and submit it successfully to Kindle. With these entrepreneurial spirited people in mind, I now present the revised version, geared specifically for submitting your work to Kindle with the bonus option of *also* submitting to Smashwords. I hope you find as much value in it as did those readers of the original.

After all of this, you will understand that my thanks go to the following: God, first and foremost. Thank you. And to my authors; if it were not for you and your compelling works, I would have never discovered the wonderful world of publishing.

# Kindle Formatting Guide for Idjits

## Taking Your Manuscript and Making it Kindle Compatible in Seven Easy Steps

Rebecca Melvin

# Chapter 1: The First Two Steps – Copy File – Remove Problems

## 1. Make a copy of your original file and save it under a new name.

Example: **My Book.doc** can be saved as **My Book - Kindle version.doc**

**If you have "Track Changes" on, unclick it now, ensure that the dropdown box reads "Final" and then do the "Save As".** (If you forget, that's okay, I'll show you how to fix it at the end).

## <u>2. Remove the following</u>:

-A-<u>**Headers and Footers**</u> (just hiding headers and footers will not work).

--If headers and footers are not showing, go to:

----View

------Headers and Footers

------Double click inside the header box and delete any text within the box including page numbers, etc.

------Repeat in the Footers box.

------When finished, click on View: Headers and Footers to again hide the now empty boxes.

## -B-<u>Hyphenation</u>

**--If you did this using the auto-hyphenate feature, go to:**

----Tools

------Language

-------Hyphenation

-------Remove the checkmark in the box next to Hyphena-

tion

-------Click Okay

**--If you hyphenated manually, go to:**

----Edit

------Replace

------Type in – (hyphen) in the "Find" box

------Leave the "Replace" box empty

------Click on "Find Next" to go to each instance through-

out the document in turn. Determine in each instance if it is a

hyphen you placed in to accommodate formatting or if it is a

needed hyphen to be grammatically correct. Remove those

placed for formatting issues. Leave the ones needed to be

grammatically correct.

### -C-<u>Tabs</u>

--Go to:

----Edit

------Replace

------Type in ^t in the "Find" box

------Leave the "Replace" box empty

------Click on "Replace All"

------Click "okay"

### -D-<u>Extra Spaces</u> (Books are not formatted like business writing. Do not leave two spaces between sentences. If you did this, they need to be removed. If you did not intentionally leave extra spaces, you should still go through this process to eliminate any that were placed in by error).

--Go to:

----Edit

------Replace

------Type two space bar spaces into the "Find" box (you will not see any characters, just the cursor moving over two spaces).

------Type one space bar space into the "Replace" box

------Click on "Replace All"

------Click "okay"

------Do this process a second time. This will ensure that if you had any three space errors, that they will now be eliminated as well as they have been reduced down to a double spacing error with the first time through.


**-E-Page Breaks** (ebooks do not support page breaks. They need to be replaced with 'returns').

--Turn on:

----"¶" (up on your tool bar). This will reveal all your formatting characters.

----Scroll through your document finding any places where there is a line showing all the way across your document. This is an inserted page break. Click your cursor at the end of the sentence immediately above it and hit "delete" until the line disappears.

----Replace where the line was with NO MORE THAN THREE RETURNS (three empty lines). Delete any remaining blank lines between the end of the previous text and the start of the next text.

----An alternate would be NO MORE THAN THREE RETURNS – then - * - or - *** - then – NO MORE THAN THREE MORE RETURNS.

# Chapter 2: Steps Three, Four and Five – In Select All

### 3.-<u>In Select All</u>:

### -A-<u>To Select All, go to:</u>

--Edit

----Select All (this will highlight your entire manuscript. Changes made now will apply to the entire work).

### -B-<u>Keep your text highlighted by Select All</u> (don't click anywhere on the text block or it will disappear and you will have to Select All again). Go to:

--Format

----Styles and Formatting

----In the scroll box that appears on the right side of your screen, scroll down until you find the formatting titled "Normal".

----Hover over Normal. It will display its current settings which should read: font: Times New Roman, 12 pt, Left

----If it does not display the above defaults, you will need to change its defaults. Do this by:

------Hover over Normal again. A drop down box arrow will appear to the right of it. Click on it to open the drop down box.

------Select "Modify"

--------If you would like to keep the original defaults under Normal for other uses, then rename this setting to **Normal Kindle** for future use by changing the Name in the "Name" box.

-------Change the settings to:

-----------Formatting:

-----------Times New Roman

-----------12 pt

-----------Left justification

-----------Single line spacing

-----------**If your work is non-fiction and you need block paragraphs instead of first line indent paragraphs, you can change this here at this time by clicking on the appropriate "increase" paragraph button.**

-------Check the box that says "Add to Template"

-------Click "Okay"

-----Hover over Normal again (or the new template name if you renamed it) to ensure that the defaults now read correctly in the information box that appears.

## 4. Check your text: is it still highlighted from Select All? If not, hit Select All again.

--Click on Normal (or the appropriate newly named format-ting style you created especially for Kindle) to update all of your text at once.


## 5. Remain in Select All (all your text is still highlighted). Go to:


--Format

----Paragraph

------First Tab: Indents and Spacing

--------Under General:

----------Alignment: Setting should be "Left"

--------Under Indentation:

----------Left: Setting should be "0"

----------Right: Setting should be "0"

----------Special: Setting should be "First Line" and the number should be "0.25" (this will give you a consistent first line indent *without* tabs or spaces!) **If you are using block paragraphs (for non-fiction) with a space in between** (accomplished at the end of step 4 above) **do NOT set a first line**

**indent.**

--------Under Spacing:

----------Before should be set to "0"

----------After should be set to "0"

----------Line Spacing should be set to "Single"

--------Click Okay

------Second Tab: Line and Page Breaks

--------Clear out all boxes. Any boxes checked need to be unchecked. To be really certain, any box that is even just showing green without a check mark, check it and then uncheck it.

--------Click Okay

# Chapter 3: Steps Six and Seven – General Clean-Up and Front Matter

**6. Click anywhere on the text block to remove the Select All feature. Your text block should no longer be highlighted. Now we are going to work on your front matter: title page, copyright, acknowledgments, dedications, etc, and chapter headings:**

--After all the previous steps, your title should appear as Times New Roman at 12 pt and is left justified. To adjust this:

----Highlight your Title and author name and your publishing house logo and address (all of what would normally appear as your 'Title Page' in the printed book).

-------Center your Title, author name and publishing house information.

-------With your title 'page' information still highlighted, go to the ruler at the top of your page. The top arrow, pointing down, will still show a first line indent of 0.25. Click and hold on the little arrow and move it to the left so that it is even with the little arrow pointing up. This will ensure that your title page information is truly centered and not a quarter of an inch off (remember we set the default at 0.25 when in "select all")

-------Increase your title page font sizes to anything appropriate at **18 pt or lower. Keeping the font to 18 pt or lower will enable you to submit you work to Smashwords as well as Kindle without having it rejected.** You can also change the font but limit it to a choice of Arial or Book Antiqua. Anything more exotic will be tossed by the Smashwords Meatgrinder.

**\* If your title is currently in ALL CAPS, Smashwords' Meatgrinder will reject it. You must have your title small**

**case with capitals only at the beginning of each word as appropriate.**

-------Remove all but three returns or less between your Title and your author name.

-------Remove all but three returns or less between your author name and your publishing logo and information. I suggest three returns, an * and then three more returns to give it more spacing and a more professional look (reference our title page at the beginning of this book for an example).

-------You need to have clear copyright infringement statement. We successfully use our standard copyright infringement statement (reference the copyright information portion at the beginning of this book). Smashwords founder Mark Coker includes a specific statement in the official Smashwords Style Guide, which is a free download, for your use also. It will also work with Kindle and will ensure that your work is not rejected by Smashwords if opting to upload to them. Either way, **a comprehensive statement must be included.**

*

Note that all spacing between the 'title page' matter, 'copyright page' matter and 'Acknowledgements, Dedication and any additional front matter' needs to be three returns or less. If you need more spacing to achieve something that is aesthetically pleasing, add an * and add more spacing, but it should be very, very limited as people reading on devices as small as their cell phone do not want 'page' after 'page' of blanks or asterisks (again, reference this book's front matter pages for an example on good spacing choices).

*

-------Scroll down through your text and make appropriate changes to additional front matter (Acknowledgments, Dedication, etc) and Chapter headers. Remember you can center Chapter Headings and change the font sizes as needed as long as they remain under 18 pt and you stick to basic fonts such as Arial or Book Antiqua. Remember to adjust the little arrow on your ruler to ensure that each is truly centered.

Note: if you begin each Chapter with the actual word "Chapter" (ex: Chapter One, Chapter Two, etc), Smashwords' Meatgrinder will automatically create Chapter Navigation for you in ePub if submitting to them.

## 7. General Clean up:

--Once again, click on ¶ in your tool bar to show formatting characters throughout your text:

----Scroll down through your text looking for anything 'weird' that may indicate tabs, page breaks, or multiple spacing. Also check that the paragraphs all look uniform with the same font, same pt size, and all left justified. Word has been known to be stubborn about thinking it knows what you want better than you do. If you find something out of the ordinary, correct it using the processes I showed you above.

----As one last precaution, and also if you forgot to turn off tracking:

-------Turn **off** the ¶ button.

-------**Hit the Save button.**

-------Click on the 'Track Changes' button.

-------In the drop down box on your toolbar, click on "Final Showing Markup".

----------Now scroll through your document looking for any text that shows up in RED or BLUE or any other color other than black.

----------IF YOU HAVE ANY COLORS OTHER THAN BLACK:

-------------Switch the drop box from Final Showing Markup to "Final" (this will make the colors go away, but guess what, when you upload to meatgrinder, they're still going to be there. Yes, it's true. I've seen it happen).

-------------With the dropbox set to "Final", do a Select All – right click your mouse, select "Copy", open a new word doc and Paste in your entire text.

-------------Check the new doc by hitting "Final Showing Markup" in the dropdown box. There should not be any changes tracked (no colored text). Save this under a new name, or overwrite it to the old name (after closing that one out after copying it).

You are now ready to upload your text block to Kindle.

Good luck! And drop me a line to let me know how this worked out for you at cuttingedge@atlanticbb.net.

**BONUS SECTION** – Taking Your Kindle text doc and making it Smashwords compatible in one additional easy step:

If you followed the steps above for uploading to Kindle, you'll note that we already did a few things that Kindle doesn't necessarily require (but that gives you a good, clean Kindle ebook by doing them anyways) but that Smashwords does require in order to achieve their Premium Catalog status (which gets your work into iBooks and Nook). That little bit of extra time and effort now pays off, because to make your Kindle ebook text block compatible with Smashwords, you only need to do one additional thing:

-------Your copyright portion **has to include your ISBN obtained through Smashwords and the words "Smashwords Edition" next to it**

To do this:

----Go to Smashwords, upload your work *without* the ISBN. I know, seems silly. Once it has uploaded, go to your Smashwords account Dashboard. Click on ISBN Manager in your left hand navigation column. Once your title has been converted, it will appear on this page, and you can use the link to obtain a free ISBN for it then. Now you have to go back to the file you just uploaded, add the ISBN and re-upload it again.

It should look like this (example):

Your Publishing House Name – Smashwords ebook edition

Ebook ISBN: 987-6-5432-1987-6

Your Kindle ebook text doc is now a Smashwords ebook text doc.

Easy-peasy-lemon-squeezy. ☺